# CAERNARFON CASTLE
## AND TOWN WALLS

### Arnold Taylor CBE, DLitt, FBA

*Contents*

*Edited by David M. Robinson BSc, PhD, FSA*
*Designed by Icon Design*

*First Published (Her Majesty's Stationery Office, London) 1953*
*This Edition: First Published (Cadw, Cardiff) 1986*
*Revised 1993; Fourth Edition 1997; Fifth Edition 2001*

© *Cadw: Welsh Historic Monuments (Crown Copyright),*
*Crown Building, Cathays Park, Cardiff, CF10 3NQ*

*Printed in Great Britain by South Western Printers*
*ISBN 1 85760 147 5*

# INTRODUCTION

*'... to Caernarvon, where I thought to have seen a Town and a Castle, or a Castle and a Town; but I saw both to be one, and one to be both; for indeed a man can hardly divide them in judgement or apprehension; and I have seen many gallant fabrics and fortifications, but for compactness and completeness of Caernarvon, I never yet saw a parallel. And it is by Art and Nature so fitted and seated, that it stands impregnable, and if it be well manned, victualled, and ammunitioned, it is invincible, except fraud or famine do assault, or conspire against it'.*

John Taylor, *A Short Relation of a Long Journey made Round or Ovall by encompassing the Principalitie of Wales, Etc.* (1652).

Caernarfon Castle, begun in 1283 and still not completely finished when building work stopped in about 1330, is one of the most striking buildings the Middle Ages have left to us. It is one of a group of imposing and majestic castles in north Wales that still remain in a state of some completeness. But Caernarfon undoubtedly stands apart from the others, in its sheer scale, in its nobility, and in the degree of its architectural finish. Small wonder, then, that this great castle should have caught the imagination of scores of writers and painters through the ages. As early as the seventeenth century, John Taylor was clearly most impressed with the stronghold at the mouth of the Seiont river, 'by Art and Nature so fitted and seated'. Over a hundred years later, Dr Samuel Johnson (1709–84) wrote in his diary that the stupendous magnitude and strength of Caernarfon surpassed his idea, for — as he said — he did not think there had been such buildings.

From the very beginning, Caernarfon Castle was conceived as a fortress-palace of some special significance. It was to be a stronghold brimming with image and symbolism. An age-old folk-memory had long associated this place with the imperial world of Rome, a tale enshrined in the well-known Macsen Wledig romance of the *Mabinogion*. King Edward I (1272–1307) chose to build on this legend. He decided to encourage his brilliant architect, Master James of St George, to design a castle which would echo the walls of the Emperor Constantine's Roman city of Constantinople. Caernarfon's 'great towers of many colours' were the crowning representation of ancient story in stone – the fairest castle that man had ever seen.

*Caernarfon Castle was begun by King Edward I of England in 1283. It was always marked out as a building of some special purpose with its architecture brimming with image and symbolism. Construction continued through to about 1330, by which time the stronghold had still not been completed to its original design.*

# A HISTORY OF THE CASTLE

*The Romans knew their fort on the River Seiont as Segontium. Its remains stand on the outskirts of the modern town of Caernarfon. The 'playing-card' shape of the fort can be clearly seen in this aerial view from the south-east. The medieval castle appears in the distance, where the river flows into the Menai Strait.*

## CAERNARFON BEFORE KING EDWARD I

Caernarfon is one of the historic centres of Wales, its remoter past already enshrined in legend when, just over seven hundred years ago, an English king chose it to be the seat of a new administration and gave it new fame as the cradle of a line of English princes. The castle and town walls, built at that time — and still in large part surviving — were successors to a Roman fortification raised more than a thousand years earlier, the ruins of which were then to be seen standing, where their foundations may yet be seen today, on the outskirts of the town astride the way to Beddgelert. Indeed, it was from this site that Caernarfon took its name; for to the Welsh the Roman fort was 'y gaer yn Arfon', the 'stronghold in the land over against Môn' — the island of Mona or Anglesey.

*A gold coin of the usurper Roman emperor, Magnus Maximus (A.D. 383–88), the Macsen Wledig of the* Mabinogion *(By permission of the National Museum & Gallery Cardiff).*

4

A variant was Caer Segeint, for the name by which the Romans knew their fort was *Segontium*, from the ancient British word for the River Seiont, close to whose bank it stood. The waters of the Seiont, sheltered and tidal at this point, had much to do with its siting and carried much of its traffic.

Little can be said with certainty or precision as to the status of Caernarfon in the six-and-a-half centuries that separate the departure of the Romans from the coming of the Normans, for history and legend are inextricably intertwined in the saga of the *Mabinogion*, in which the glory of *Segontium* is the background for historical characters in heroic guise. Apart from the sheltering haven of the Seiont itself, only one link connects that almost vanished age with later and better known times. This is the site and dedication of Llanbeblig church, situated, not on the outskirts of medieval Caernarfon, but on Roman *Segontium*, yet continuing to this day as the mother church of the whole town. Peblig, whose name is derived from the Roman Publicius, is reputed to have been one of the sons of Magnus Maximus, emperor of Gaul, Spain and Britain from A.D. 383 to 388, the Macsen Wledig of the *Mabinogion*. In this church, and the buildings which preceded it, Christian worship has maintained continuity from the fifth century until our own time.

*The mother church of Caernarfon (Llanbeblig) is dedicated to St Peblig, a name derived from the Roman Publicius, and reputed to have been one of the sons of Magnus Maximus.*

*An imaginative reconstruction of the Roman fort of* Segontium, *in about A.D. 250, viewed from the east. The drawing is based upon archaeological excavations in 1921–23 and 1975–79 (Illustration by John Banbury, 1996).*

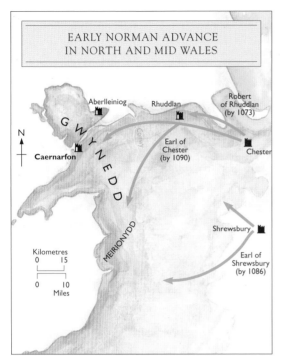

EARLY NORMAN ADVANCE
IN NORTH AND MID WALES

With the Norman Conquest, sealed by the coronation of William I (1066–87) at Westminster on Christmas Day 1066, we pass from obscurity to relatively well-recorded fact. The new rulers of England lost little time in seeking to bring the regions of Wales under Anglo-Norman military and political control. Already by 1073 a certain Robert, a kinsman of Hugh of Avranches (d. 1101), the first Norman earl of Chester, had established a castle, borough and mint at Rhuddlan and gained control of the northern coastlands up to the line of the River Conwy.

*A silver penny minted at Rhuddlan late in the reign of the Conqueror (By permission of the National Museum & Gallery Cardiff).*

*Robert of Rhuddlan (d. 1088) established a motte and bailey castle at Rhuddlan on the River Clwyd by 1073. This artist's impression shows how the stronghold may have appeared in the late eleventh century. Robert's kinsman, Earl Hugh of Chester (d. 1101), raised a similar castle at Caernarfon (Illustration by Terry Ball, 1989).*

*Right: By 1115, the Welsh princes had recovered their losses in Gwynedd and were to retain Caernarfon until 1283. This manuscript illustration is taken from a mid thirteenth-century copy of the great Welsh law book of Hywel Dda — Hywel the Good (d. 950) — and depicts a Welsh prince as lawgiver (By courtesy of the National Library of Wales, Peniarth Ms. 28, f. 1v).*

By the time of the Domesday Survey (1086) this Robert of Rhuddlan — as he was called — had been granted a nominal lieutenancy over the whole of north Wales, but it was left to the earl himself, after Robert's death at Welsh hands in 1088, to carry effective Norman power into Gwynedd. About the year 1090, he established castles at Aberlleiniog in Anglesey, at Caernarfon, and at a site not yet certainly identified in the Welsh *cantref* or district of Meirionydd.

Earl Hugh placed his castle at Caernarfon at the water's edge, on the peninsula formed by the estuary of the Seiont, the Menai Strait and the Cadnant brook. This eleventh-century castle was of the motte and bailey type, with steep earthen banks and heavy timber palisading. Its dominant feature, a circular mound, or motte, was later incorporated within the upper or eastern ward of the Edwardian castle, there to survive in a modified form until after 1870. The position occupied by Earl Hugh's bailey is less certain; probably it lay to the north-east of the motte and included part of the open ground later known as the Prince's Garden and now represented by Castle Square. As to the buildings associated with the earthworks, it is likely that there would have been a tower on the mound and that at first this would have been a timber structure; but it would be unwise to assume that it necessarily remained so through the succeeding two centuries.

Nor should we suppose that no stone buildings were erected by the Welsh princes, who having recovered their losses in Gwynedd by 1115, retained possession of Caernarfon until the final collapse of native power in 1283. We know from documents dated there that Llywelyn ab Iorwerth — Llywelyn the Great (d. 1240) — sometimes resided at Caernarfon, as did his grandson Llywelyn ap Gruffudd — Llywelyn the Last (d. 1282) — later in the thirteenth century. We know, too, that around the royal court or *llys* there lay a typical Welsh *maenor*, whose territory included most of Llanbeblig, with other neighbouring hamlets, and whose townsmen, with agricultural holdings in the surrounding fields, were the predecessors of the English burgesses settled on their lands under charter from King Edward I.

*Below: This carved stone head, possibly representing Llywelyn the Great (1173–1240), was found at Deganwy Castle. There was a Welsh royal court or llys at Caernarfon, and from documents we know that Prince Llywelyn sometimes resided there (By permission of the National Museum & Gallery Cardiff).*

*Accused of being an autocratic and short-tempered man, King Edward I of England (1272–1307) possessed an undoubted talent for leadership. Following his second war with Llywelyn ap Gruffudd, prince of Wales, the king ordered the construction of Caernarfon Castle in 1283. This late thirteenth-century manuscript illustration shows Edward seated and holding a sword. He faces his archbishops and a group of clergy with scribes at their feet (By kind permission of the British Library, Cotton Vitellius Ms. A XIII, f. 6v).*

# THE BUILDING OF THE TOWN AND CASTLE
## FIRST PHASE: 1283-1292

In the year 1283 we enter on a new era. From this date onwards the survival of contemporary records, though but a fraction of those originally kept, enables us to follow the growth of the buildings we now see and to reconstruct the different stages of the work with reasonable confidence. Since Palm Sunday (22 March) 1282, there had been war, for the second time in five years, between King Edward I of England, and Llywelyn, prince of Wales. In December 1282, Llywelyn was killed near Builth, and then on 18 January the English capture of Dolwyddelan Castle, the key to Snowdonia and hub of its communications, opened the way through the Conwy valley, the Llanberis Pass and the Vale of Ffestiniog, to Conwy, Caernarfon and Harlech.

The king himself arrived at Conwy on or about 14 March, and the construction of Conwy Castle

'Know, sir,' read the dispatch sent to King Edward in December 1282, 'that Llywelyn ap Gruffudd is dead, his army broken, and all the flower of his men killed'. The prince died in or after a substantial skirmish a few miles from Builth. This manuscript depiction of the event may reflect the English bias of its source (By permission of the British Library, Cotton Nero Ms. D II, f. 182).

was begun immediately. The fall of Castell y Bere (north-west of Tywyn) on 25 April secured the southern flank of the English advance, while the capture of Dolbadarn, probably sometime in May, denied Llywelyn's brother, Dafydd (d. 1283), his last remaining stronghold. Within a few weeks the works begun at Conwy in March were being paralleled at Caernarfon and Harlech, and, in the years that followed, this great trio of castles, conceived on a scale which over-shadowed even the might of those so recently built at Flint, Rhuddlan and Aberystwyth, rose with astonishing speed to embrace and grip the intractable heart of northern Wales.

Here we are only concerned with Caernarfon. From the beginning, the castle, the town with its wall and gates, and the quay to which most of the heavy building materials were brought by water, were pushed forward as parts of a single operation. The building of one was to some extent dependent on the building of the others. All, so far as we can now judge, were begun more or less simultaneously in the summer of 1283.

The very first recorded reference to the building works (24 June) mentions the new castle ditch, which would separate the castle from the streets and houses to the north. Next, as was done during the building of other north Wales castles, a *bretagium* or barricade was erected to fence in and protect the site of the new works. Great quantities of timber were shipped from Conwy, Rhuddlan and Liverpool, and

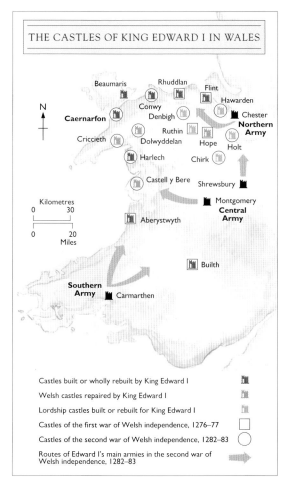

### THE CASTLES OF KING EDWARD I IN WALES

N

Beaumaris
Rhuddlan
Flint
Caernarfon
Conwy
Denbigh
Hawarden
Chester
**Northern Army**
Criccieth
Ruthin
Dolwyddelan
Hope
Holt
Harlech
Chirk
Castell y Bere
Shrewsbury

Kilometres
0    30

0    20
Miles

Montgomery
**Central Army**
Aberystwyth

Builth

**Southern Army**
Carmarthen

Castles built or wholly rebuilt by King Edward I

Welsh castles repaired by King Edward I

Lordship castles built or rebuilt for King Edward I

Castles of the first war of Welsh independence, 1276–77

Castles of the second war of Welsh independence, 1282–83

Routes of Edward I's main armies in the second war of Welsh independence, 1282–83 use was also made of wood from the pontoon bridge by which, not many months earlier, an ill-starred English force had crossed from Anglesey, only to be annihilated on the Bangor shore. Diggers in their hundreds, besides excavating the castle moat, levelled platforms in the rock and cut the great foundation trenches required for walls some of which at their base are nearly 20 feet (6m) thick. Where houses of the old Welsh township lay in the way, they were demolished and their timber impounded, compensation not being paid till three years later. On the site of the future castle, substantial timber-framed apartments were erected for the accommodation of King Edward and his queen, Eleanor. They arrived from Conwy on 11 or 12 July and stayed for more than a month before continuing their journey through Bala, Ruthin and Chester to Shrewsbury and Acton Burnell.

Preparatory work went on during the winter, and by the time Edward and Eleanor came again to Caernarfon the following Easter much progress must have been made. Indeed, it is not impossible that the Eagle Tower, which alone of all the towers can be shown to have been built complete and entire from front to rear from the first, could, if the earliest effort was concentrated on it, have already been carried up to first-floor level. If so, the tradition that it was here that the birth — on 25 April 1284 — of their son Edward of Caernarfon took place may indeed by a well-grounded one.

# ARCHITECT AND BUILDERS

*In this mid thirteenth-century manuscript illustration by Matthew Paris, a king is shown directing his master mason. In the background, builders are busy with construction work (By permission of the British Library, Cotton Nero Ms. D I, f. 23v).*

*A section from the accounts of payments to building workers at Caernarfon in 1284. The workers were preparing accommodation in readiness for the king and queen (Copyright: Public Record Office, E 101/351/9).*

It can be said with reasonable certainty that the architect of Caernarfon Castle was James of St George (about 1235–1308), a highly paid master mason and military engineer whose services, as master of the king's works in Wales, Edward I secured by arrangement with Count Philip of Savoy (1268–85) before March 1278. Prior to that, James had been employed successively by Count Peter II (1263–68) and Philip of Savoy as their chief household architect, in which capacity he had had at least sixteen years' experience directing castle and other works in all parts of their Alpine dominion, from the Rhône east to Turin and from the Lake of Neuchâtel south to beyond the Mont Cenis. James took his surname from Philip's palace of St Georges d'Esperanche, which had been built under his direction between 1268 and 1274, and it was at St Georges that he probably resided until his transfer to Edward I's service early in 1278. He controlled, besides the works at Caernarfon, the building of Conwy, Harlech and Beaumaris, along with Flint, Rhuddlan, Aberystwyth and Builth; he also directed works at Hope in 1282 and later at Criccieth, Bere and

By now the new moat was ready to receive its turf revetment, lime was being supplied to the castle, and stone was being ferried across from Anglesey. In this spring and summer of 1284 the castle we now see must have been beginning to take visible shape; the construction of the town walls was also progressing, and by the end of 1285 it was substantially complete. Very heavy expenditure in the 1286 building season shows that work on the castle was continuing unabated. In 1287 the high proportion of expenditure assigned to 'task' or piece work is an indication that the chief emphasis was by that time no longer on the mass employment of masons and labourers, but rather on the 'fitting out' and on particular jobs more easily handled by smaller groups of craftsmen. In the 1288 season, works expenditure, though still appreciable, was not a tenth of what it had been. In the three following seasons it was negligible, and after 1292 the accounts cease altogether.

Dolwyddelan; he may also have had at least supervisory responsibility for the castles of Denbigh, Ruthin, Holt, Hawarden and Chirk.

Master James's staff probably also included assistant masons and engineers brought from the Continent. Under this small nucleus, a veritable army of quarriers and stone-cutters, masons, smiths and carpenters, plumbers and labourers, all drawn from every shire in England and led by English masters, carried on the actual work of construction.

*King Edward I and Queen Eleanor depicted in a miniature manuscript illustration. They arrived at the castle works in Caernarfon on 11 or 12 July 1283 and stayed in comfortable timber-framed apartments for more than a month (By kind permission of the British Library, Cotton Nero Ms. D II, f. 179v).*

*A plan of 1794 showing the castle of St Georges d'Esperanche. Caernarfon's architect, Master James of St George, took his surname from this fortress-palace of the counts of Savoy. Master James directed the works there from 1268 until 1274, before his service was transferred to King Edward I (By courtesy of the Archives de l'Isère).*

THE ORIGINS OF THE LABOUR FORCE FOR
KING EDWARD I'S CASTLE-BUILDING IN WALES

Numbers of Workmen Conscripted

Carpenters
Diggers
Masons

Gathering points

New castles under construction

Counties so marked also provided some 1,600 woodcutters

# THE BIRTH OF A PRINCE

To some extent, Caernarfon's future status was determined on 25 April 1284 by the birth of a prince within the castle precincts. On his ten-year-old brother Alfonso's death four months later, the infant was to become King Edward I's eldest surviving son. It was not, however, until 1301 that Edward of Caernarfon, as he was named from his birthplace, was formally created prince of Wales and endowed with the rule and revenues of all the Crown's Welsh lands. From that date the title has normally been accorded to the eldest son of the reigning monarch.

Whether or not one of the intentions of the formal act of 1301 was to give legal effect to an earlier nomination, traditionally supposed to have been made to the Welsh nobility in the year of his birth, of a prince 'that was borne in Wales and could speak never a word of English', will perhaps never be known. The story is one that cannot be traced in writing until three hundred years later, but it is not inherently improbable and may well embody a genuine tradition. At all events, no episode is more widely associated with Caernarfon in popular thought. In 1911, when processes undreamt of in 1300 had placed among the king's chief ministers at Westminster a Welshman, namely David Lloyd George (1863–1945), elected to represent the constituency of Caernarfon Boroughs, the castle became for the first time the scene of a ceremonial Royal Investiture

*Traditionally, King Edward I presented his infant son to the people of Wales as a prince 'borne in Wales and could speake never a word of English'. David Powel's* The Historie of Cambria *(1584) includes the earliest know reference to this proclamation tale (By permission of the National Museum & Gallery Cardiff).*

*In this manuscript illustration, Edward of Caernarfon, later King Edward II (1307–27), is created prince of Wales by his father in 1301 (By permission of the British Library, Cotton Ms. Nero D II, f. 191v).*

which clothed the forms and memories of the past in modern pageantry, and thereby furthered in this respect Caernarfon's claims to primacy among the towns of Wales. In 1963 Her Majesty the Queen conferred upon it the title and status of a Royal Borough, and in 1969 the Investiture of Prince Charles as prince of Wales took place in the castle following the precedent established in 1911.

---

By this date there had been spent on the castle, town walls and related works a sum totalling approximately £12,000. This was a vast outlay, but was not disproportionate to the achievement. The town walls were probably finished, and the whole external southern façade and east end of the castle, from the Eagle Tower round to the North-East Tower, had been built to a good height. Together, the town walls and southern face of castle formed a complete and defensible enclosure.

Construction of the north side of the castle, which was within the covering protection of the walled town and therefore not exposed to direct attack, was less urgent. The castle was protected on this side by the great ditch hewn out at the very commencement of the work in 1283–84, a more formidable obstacle than might appear from the narrowed form in which it exists today. Consequently, as we can deduce from a contemporary record, the northern curtains had only been built to a height varying between 12 feet (3.6m) and 24 feet (7.3m) above the bottom of the ditch by the time work was about to be taken up again in the spring of 1296. By then the northern towers had also certainly been begun, but we do not know to what height they had been carried.

# THE 1294 REVOLT AND THE SECOND BUILDING PHASE: 1294-1330

With building proceeding apace, Caernarfon's future legal and governmental roles were cast in March 1284. Under the Statute of Wales or Rhuddlan (as it is alternatively known), among other matters of legislation, the three shires of Gwynedd — Anglesey, Caernarvon and Merioneth — were established as a single administrative unit. The new borough of Caernarfon was to be the county town of one of them, and was to serve as the centre of government for the whole.

A decade later, with building of the castle and town having reached the stage described above, the Welsh broke into widespread and open revolt. Edward I was taken completely by surprise. Almost the whole of the country was affected, with the 'national' leader, Madog ap Llywelyn, assuming the title 'prince of Wales'. Caernarfon, both the symbol and centre of the new order, was overrun, and the sheriff, one of the officers established by the Statute of 1284, was assassinated.

Very heavy damage was done to the new town wall, and once this barrier had been passed little more than the wooden *bretagium* and the moat would have hindered the insurgents from swarming into the castle itself. Once they were inside, everything combustible was put to the flame. Our own narrative itself suffers from the loss of records known to have been destroyed at this time.

The king's response was swift and devastating. By the following summer, in a vigorous reaction, the English had recovered what had been lost. Orders were given for putting the town of Caernarfon in a state of defence again not later than 11 November 1295. This involved work at high pressure, and two months before the target date the rebuilding of the town walls had been completed at a cost of £1,195. This sum, nearly half the original recorded cost of the walls, shows that in places the damage must have amounted to complete destruction. This would seem to confirm that contemporary references to the town walls having been 'thrown down' by the Welsh rebels (*muri ville ... per Wallenses ... prostrati*) were not exaggerated. Next, the repair of the castle damage was taken in hand and preparations made to resume work on a major scale in the following February on the parts still unfinished.

*This imaginative reconstruction depicts the town and castle of Caernarfon, as Madog ap Llywelyn's rebels burst through the defences in September 1294. At the time of the assault, the town walls appear to have stood very substantially complete. It seems, however, that building works on the north curtain wall and towers of the castle had not progressed to such an extent. These areas are unlikely to have risen much beyond the level of their footings (Illustration by Ivan Lapper, 1993).*

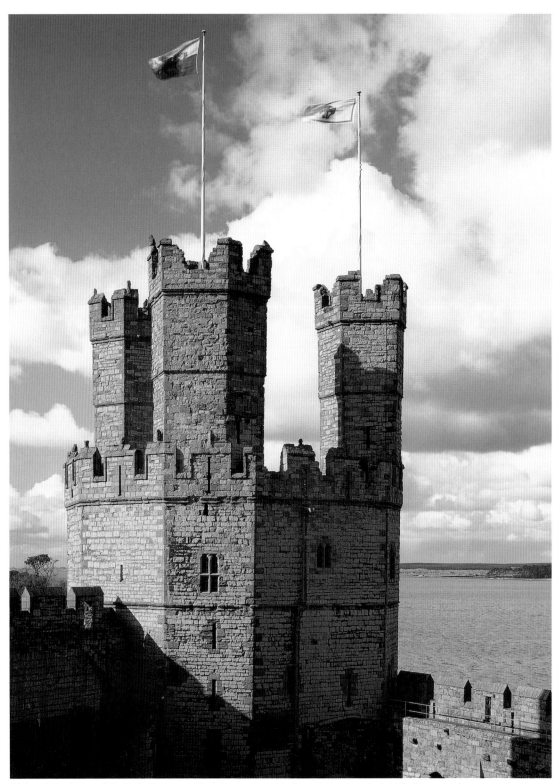

*Although the design of the Eagle Tower was doubtless envisaged in its entirety when the initial plans were drawn up, there is evidence that it was left with a temporary roof in the later 1280s. The addition of the fourth storey, together with the three crowning turrets, accounted for further major expenditure at the castle in the early fourteenth century.*

*This detail from a late-medieval German manuscript shows men hoisting materials to the top of an angular tower by crane. Workers are busy cutting stone and mixing mortar on the ground. A wooden scaffold supports the masons laying the stones. The scenes are doubtless little different from those at Caernarfon in the early fourteenth century (By kind permission of the Württembergische Landesbibliothek, Stuttgart, Cod. Bibl. 2'5, f. 9v).*

Events had demonstrated that completion of the townward side was, after all, vital, and a document has survived suggesting that this was the section on which work was first resumed. Between July 1294 and the end of 1301 nearly £4,500 was expended on the castle works. Probably by the latter date the building up of the four lengths of curtain wall linking the Eagle and the North-East Towers had made good progress, and it is fair to presume that at least the outer faces of the intervening towers would also by this time have been carried up to an equivalent height. The vaulted passage of the King's Gate, together with its elaborate defences (pp. 26–27), and the arrowslits grouped to give maximum fire-power from the curtain walls to the east, are of this period and later. All reflect the sense of insecurity left by the recent disaster.

In 1301–02 orders were given to rebuild in stone the wooden bridge by which, prior to 1294, the main gate of the town had been approached across the Cadnant (p. 42). Then, between

November 1301 and September 1304, there is a gap in the accounts. This may mean that building at the castle had been largely brought to a standstill by the transfer of labour to the war in Scotland. Walter of Hereford, the master mason who had had charge of the works since 1295, was certainly in Scotland during the years in question, but after Edward's victory at Stirling in 1304 it was possible to take up work once again on the unfinished buildings at Caernarfon.

Work was resumed in the autumn of 1304 and we know that approximately £700 was spent in each of the next two years. Expenditure of this order allowed the employment of seventy to a hundred men in the winter months and 150 to 200 in the summer. Though details are lacking, there is no reason to suppose that progress was not maintained at something like this level through the three following years also. From 1309 until 1330, and very possibly for a few years longer, building went steadily on, but on nothing like the scale reached in the 1280s and after the 1294 revolt. Proportionately to the whole building, we should expect to assign relatively little new construction to these final years, and there are documents which help us to say what it was.

In 1316 the timber-framed 'Hall of Llywelyn', part of the last Welsh prince's residence at Conwy, was dismantled and shipped to Caernarfon, where it was re-erected within the castle. In 1317 the Eagle Tower was nearing completion, and a carved stone eagle was being affixed on it. There is evidence in the building itself that in the 1280s the tower had been left with a temporary roof at what ultimately became the level of its top floor. The addition of the fourth storey and the three turrets — all no doubt envisaged in the original plans — was a major task, and must have accounted for a high proportion of the later expenditure.

*In 1316–17 the Eagle Tower was finally nearing completion. This section from an account of 1316 details a payment to Robert the smith who was engaged in some of the works. Robert received 14d. for making 140 roof nails, 140 clench nails, and for mending the workmens' tools. He was also to wrought three iron cramps for fixing a stone eagle on the 'great tower' — the Eagle Tower (Copyright: Public Record Office, E 101/486/29).*

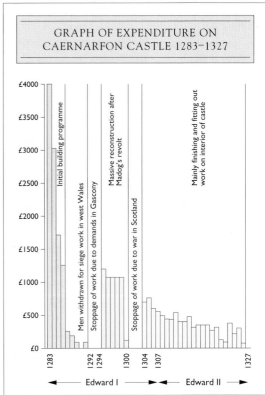

GRAPH OF EXPENDITURE ON
CAERNARFON CASTLE 1283–1327

- Initial building programme
- Men withdrawn for siege work in west Wales
- Stoppage of work due to demands in Gascony
- Massive reconstruction after Madog's revolt
- Stoppage of work due to war in Scotland
- Mainly finishing and fitting out work on interior of castle

◄— Edward I —► ◄— Edward II —►

*For parts of the year 1316–17, week-by-week particulars survive to provide a vivid picture of the building efforts during the later stages of construction at Caernarfon (Copyright: Public Record Office, E 101/486/29).*

Another piece of work belonging to this period is the upper part of the curtain wall linking the Eagle and the Queen's Towers. A third is the upper portion of the King's Gate. We learn from the accounts that the statue of Edward of Caernarfon — by this time King Edward II (1307–27) — was being erected here in 1321. In the same year oak beams 32 feet (9.6m) long, from the woods in the Conwy valley, were being obtained to floor the hall above the gate. Probably one of the last works undertaken was the rearward extension of the western gate tower; this was apparently designed to be the first instalment of a scheme which, if completed, would virtually have trebled the defences of the entrance, with subsidiary gates and portcullises opening east and west towards the respective baileys from a central octagonal space. That more of it was built than now remains is almost certain.

Speaking broadly, by 1330, when regular building payments cease to be recorded, the structure of the castle had been carried to much the state in which we see it today. Subsequent works of which we have record were of no more than a minor character. The total expenditure from 1283 onwards had been from £20,000 to £25,000, its outlay being spread over nearly fifty years. It includes the cost

Above: *In all, the building works at Caernarfon were spread over a period of almost fifty years. By 1330, the structures had been carried to their maximum extent, though some parts of the castle were left unfinished. This imaginative reconstruction shows the borough, the stone quay, and the castle itself, as they may have appeared with the works complete in the early fourteenth century (Illustration by Ivan Lapper, 1993).*

Right: *The upper portion of the King's Gate was one of the last sections of the castle to see building works. In 1321, a statue of 'Edward of Caernarfon' — by then King Edward II (1307–27) — was being erected on the gate. The king's tomb effigy rests in Gloucester Cathedral (By courtesy of the Conway Library, Courtauld Institute of Art).*

of building not only the castle itself, but also the town wall with its gates, towers and multi-arched bridge approach, the quay and other works, as well as the extensive reparations made necessary by the damage of Madog's rising and of an accidental fire which swept the town in 1304. Even so, much that was planned in the castle was never undertaken. The Queen's Gate, the outer façade of which was almost certainly completed in the 1280s, was left unfinished at the back. The toothing on the North-East and Granary Towers is an indication of unbuilt wings, two storeys high, against the adjacent curtain walls. A massive foundation, projecting inwards from the wall between the Black and Chamberlain Towers, suggests that it was proposed to enclose this side of the Norman mound with a wall which would probably have connected with buildings at the back of the King's Gate.

*When C. C. Pyne (1802–78) produced this watercolour in the nineteenth century, the character of the medieval quayside and the Eagle Tower had scarcely altered from their foundation (By courtesy of the Victoria and Albert Museum).*

# LATER HISTORY

For two hundred years the political arrangements established by the Statute of Wales in 1284 remained in force, and walled towns such as Caernarfon continued to be closed to all but English burgesses. The accession to the English throne, in 1485 of a king of Welsh lineage, in the person of Henry Tudor — King Henry VII (1485–1509) — opened the way to concessions in this respect to the Welsh-speaking population. Fifty years later, this also led to a measure of assimilation of the governmental system of Wales to that of England. Until the time of these changes, the castle continued to be maintained and garrisoned, and successfully withstood sieges by Owain Glyn Dŵr and his French allies in 1403 and 1404. Town and castle together formed the effective capital of north Wales, providing at once a safe residence for government officials and a centre for their activities.

Tudor rule, by softening old hostilities and promoting peaceful intercourse with England, diminished the need for English castles in Wales. From the sixteenth century onwards, therefore, these great buildings were increasingly neglected, and in 1538 Caernarfon, with the rest, was reported as *'moche ruynous and ferre in decaye for lakke of tymely reparations'*.

The walls, then as now, were *'exceeding good'*, but the lead work on the roofs of several of the towers had seen no major renewal for centuries; it had resulted in rotten timbers crashing through the floors below. In 1620, only the Eagle Tower and the King's Gate were still roofed and leaded, the ground-floor rooms on either side of the latter having long been used as county prisons, the one for felons and the other for debtors. As for the buildings within the castle, they were *'all quite faln down to the ground and the Tymber and the rest of the materialls as Iron and Glasse carryed away and nothing left that [is] valiable'*.

Such was the condition of a building which, in the Civil War (1642–48), was once more garrisoned for the king and thrice besieged. But to external appearance little was amiss, and after the war, as before it, a sensitive observer could not but be enraptured by the strength and perfection of the fortifications. There were others, however, who only saw them as a source of trouble, and in 1660 the government gave order for the castle and town walls to be dismantled and demolished at the expense of the county, the cost to be defrayed as far as possible from the sale of the materials. Local authority readily agreed, 'conceiving it to be for the great advantage of ourselves and posterity to have the Castle of Caernarvon and the strengthes thereof demolished'. Perhaps the 'strengthes thereof' prevailed, for demolition, if indeed it was ever started, cannot have proceeded far, and posterity is still happily free to decide whether the destruction of a monument of a grandeur unsurpassed in Wales, if not in Britain, would after all have been so greatly to its advantage.

*King Henry VII (Henry Tudor), from his gilt-bronze tomb effigy in Westminster Abbey. Henry's accession to the throne in 1485 opened the way to concessions for the Welsh-speaking population in boroughs such as Caernarfon (By courtesy of the Dean and Chapter of Westminster).*

*John, Lord Byron — the last fighting constable of Caernarfon. The castle was garrisoned for King Charles during the Civil War of 1642–48, and it was Byron who finally surrendered Caernarfon to the Parliamentarians in 1646 (By courtesy of the University of Manchester, Tabley House Collection).*

*Above: Hitherto unknown prosperity came to the port of Caernarfon in the early nineteenth century. It was in 1827–28 that a narrow-gauge railway linked the new 'slate quay', seen in this lithograph of 1830, to the nearby Gloddfarlon slate quarries (By courtesy of the National Library of Wales).*

*Right: In 1843, a Caernarfon ship-owner was offering emigrants a chance to sail direct to the United States in his barque the* Hindoo, *with a ballast of slates (By courtesy of Caernarfon Public Library).*

Caernarfon having thus escaped disaster, the eighteenth-century engravers, such as the brothers Buck (1742) and John Boydell of Hawarden (1750), were able to take pleasure in depicting a town and castle whose site, character and setting had in essentials scarcely altered from their foundation. The change to modern conditions did not set in till the very end of the century. New roads, the first since Roman days, were built, and the north Wales slate industry was then expanding to serve both home and overseas markets.

Hitherto unknown prosperity came to the port in 1827–28. It was at this time that George (1781–1848) and Robert Stephenson (1803–59) constructed a narrow-gauge railway to bring to the new 'slate quay' below the castle the products of the Gloddfarlon quarries at Nantlle, ten miles (16km) away. The slate trade, more than any other single factor, accounted for a rise in Caernarfon's population from less than 4,000 in 1801 to more than 10,000 in 1851. In 1843 a local ship-owner, with offices in the High Street, was even inviting emigrants to sail direct from Caernarfon to New York in his fast 600-ton sailing barque *Hindoo*, 'with a ballast of slates'. In 1852 the town was connected by standard-gauge railway to the main London, Chester and Holyhead line; this meant further expansion of the slate trade, while for Caernarfon itself the new means of communication marked the end of the era of isolation and self-sufficiency.

It was at this time of growing contact with a world beyond the limits of north Wales that the castle began to be rescued from the neglect of centuries, and a programme of repairs undertaken at government expense. The work thus begun was pursued with vigour in the last thirty years of the nineteenth century under the direction of the

*Under the direction of Sir Llewelyn Turner (1823–1903), who served as deputy-constable of Caernarfon in the late nineteenth century, the castle began to be rescued from centuries of neglect.*

as a historic building under the supervision of the Ancient Monuments Branch of that Office and its successors. The duties are currently the responsibility of Cadw: Welsh Historic Monuments on behalf of the National Assembly for Wales.

Further repairs were undertaken in connection with the Investiture ceremony in 1911, and the massive ceilings in the principal towers, following the evidence of those that had been there originally, are of this period. The town walls, having become annexed to and, for much of their length, obscured by the various properties built against them (for the most part in the early years of the nineteenth century), have also been opened up again. Their clearance was completed in 1963, and they are now treated as a monument deserving the same care and appreciation as the castle.

In 1987, Caernarfon Castle and the town walls were inscribed on the World Heritage List as an historic site of outstanding universal value.

deputy-constable, Sir Llewelyn Turner (1823–1903). He renewed the stone steps and newels in several of the towers, restored battlements, repaired the Chamberlain Tower, completed the top of the Well Tower, floored and roofed the Queen's Tower, and — in the teeth of local opposition — cleared out the northern moat and removed a clutter of unsightly encroachments from against the outer walls.

Turner's new ashlar work is readily distinguishable by the buff colour and fine grain of the material employed, a sandstone from the neighbourhood of Mostyn in Clwyd. The appearance of the castle today owes much to his vision and pertinacity.

In 1908 control of the castle, which has always remained the property of the Crown, was transferred from the Office of Woods and Forests (which had become the responsible department in 1832) to the Office of Works. Since then it has been maintained

*The construction of seating formed part of the preparations for the Investiture of Prince Edward at Caernarfon Castle in 1911. The ceremony also prompted further repairs to the medieval masonry.*

**15 Tower 4 to Tower 5** – *The best-preserved section of the town walls, with traces of battlements and arrowslits (p. 42).*

**16 St Mary's Church** – *Built inside the town walls in the early fourteenth century (p. 43).*

**17 West Gate** – *Facing the Menai Strait, it is known in Welsh as the 'Porth-yr-Aur' (p. 43).*

**18 Quay** – *Along this fine unbroken stretch of the town walls, this was built in the fourteenth century to replace the earlier wooden quay, which was burnt in the troubles of 1294–95 (p. 43).*

**14 East Gate** – *The principal landward entrance to the town. The rooms above the gate were used to accommodate the Exchequer, which from 1284 served as the administrative and financial centre of the new counties of Anglesey, Caernarvon and Merioneth (p. 42).*

**13 Town Walls** – *The circuit of the walls and towers enclosing the medieval borough has survived unbroken and extends for a distance of about 800 yards (734m), with eight towers and two twin-towered gateways (pp. 41–4).*

**12 Arrowslits** – *Multiple groupings of arrowslits can be seen in the curtain wall on either side of the Granary Tower (p. 37).*

**11 North-East Tower** – *This is of two storeys only, and around its northern face it is possible to see the break between the first and second building phases at the castle (p. 37).*

**10 Watch Tower** – *A look-out point with a lean-to roof to give cover to the watchman (p. 37).*

**1 King's Gate** – *This great twin-towered gatehouse demonstrates the immense strength of medieval fortification. If completed, it would have been defended by a drawbridge, five doors, six portcullises and numerous 'murder-holes' and arrowslits (pp. 26–7).*

# A BIRD'S-EYE VIEW OF CAERNARFON CASTLE
## AND TOWN WALLS
### FROM THE SOUTH-WEST

**2 Kitchens** – *The slight stone foundations suggest that as built the castle kitchens may have been relatively flimsy structures. The remains include interesting details of water engineering (p. 28).*

**3 Well Tower** – *The well is nearly 50 feet (15m) deep. Had the castle been completed, a gateway in the basement would have allowed water-borne supplies to be brought into the site (p. 29).*

**4 Eagle Tower** – *The greatest of all the castle's towers, with fine apartments on each of the three floors above the basement antechamber (pp. 30–2).*

**5 Queen's Tower** – *Three storeys high, this tower has a roof turret which is slightly larger than others in the castle, and originally carried a flagstaff. In the fourteenth century it was known as the Banner Tower (p. 33).*

**6 Curtain Walls** – *Horizontal bands of different coloured stone resemble one of the best-known monuments of imperial Rome — the city walls of Constantinople (p. 39).*

**7 Chamberlain Tower** – *The battlements and cresting on the tower are original, although those on the turret have been restored. This tower has the only surviving chimney in the castle (p. 34).*

**8 Cistern Tower** – *Above the roof vault is the open stone-lined rainwater tank from which the tower takes its name (p. 35).*

**9 Queen's Gate** – *The gate-passage, high above the street outside, was originally reached by a great stone-built ramp. The rear of the gate was never completed (p. 35).*

*(Illustration by John Banbury)*

23

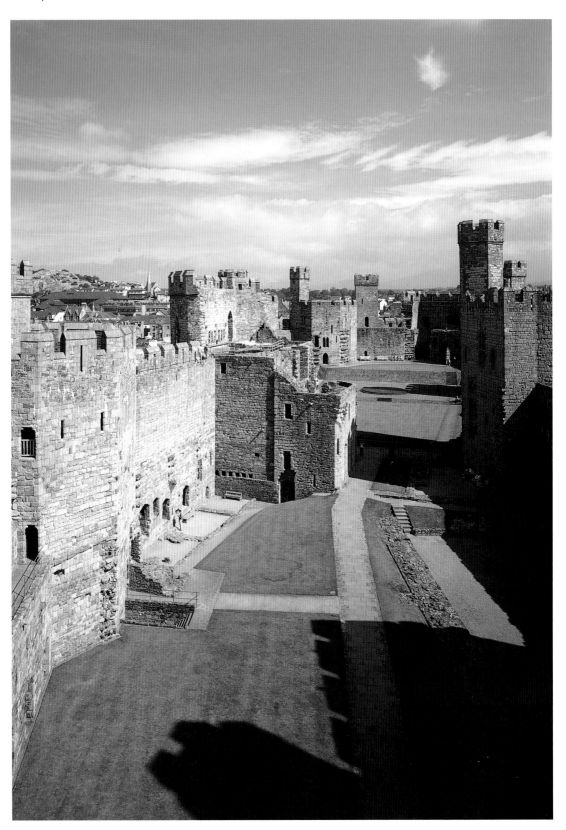

# A TOUR OF THE CASTLE

TOUR ROUTE OF THE CASTLE

N

Well Tower

King's Gate

Granary Tower

North-East Tower

Lower Ward

Upper Ward

Ward

Eagle Tower

Chamberlain Tower

Black Tower

Queen's Gate

Queen's Tower

Metres
0          30

0                    100
                    Feet

with some restoration at the wall heads, and with timber floors inserted in the larger towers around 1911. The courtyard buildings, however, have disappeared except for foundations or toothing projecting from the curtain walls. Some of the buildings, such as the back parts of the Queen's Gate, and perhaps of the King's Gate, were probably never completed, while others, such as the kitchens, may not have been built as originally intended, or were never built at all.

This tour will take you around the castle and town walls, describing the main features of interest. It is not essential to follow the route as set out, and you may prefer to make your own way around using the 'bird's-eye view' at the centre of the guide or the plan at the back. This particular tour of the castle, however, starts at the main entrance to the site (the King's Gate), and guides you around the interior in an anti-clockwise direction. We will visit each of the towers in turn, eventually returning to the point of departure. When you leave the castle, you may wish to turn right for the circuit of the town walls, ending up at the castle car-park by the river. Or, if preferred, you can turn left and return direct to the car-park.

*Left: The overall plan of Caernarfon Castle is shaped rather like a 'figure eight', divided into two wards at the waist. This view looks along the full interior length of the stronghold, with the lower ward in the foreground, the narrower waist at the centre, and the upper ward in the distance.*

*Right: An aerial view of the castle and walled town from the south.*

## THE CASTLE PLAN

The plan of the castle is shaped rather like a 'figure eight', originally divided into two at the waist with a lower ward to the right (west) of the main entrance and an upper ward to the left (east). In general terms, towers and connecting curtain walls survive largely complete, albeit

*A silver penny of King Edward I (1272–1307), the builder of Caernarfon Castle (By courtesy of the Yorkshire Museum, York).*

# THE KING'S GATE

No building in Britain demonstrates more strikingly the immense strength of medieval fortification than the great twin-towered gateway to Caernarfon Castle. Had the gatehouse been fully completed, the intruder would have had to cross a drawbridge, pass through five doors and under six portcullises, with a right-angled turn as he passed from the main gate-passage to a smaller passage, before entering the lower ward over a second drawbridge. Arrowloops and spy holes flank and command the approach from different levels, while in the vaulting above there are groups of 'murder-holes' to threaten assailants, and from which water could be poured down to extinguish any fire that might be started against the gates. Evidence for all these features is preserved in the walls, although the main bridge pit and its bearings are concealed by the modern wooden decking. Beyond the line of the third portcullis, doors on either side lead to the porters' rooms.

As you leave the gatehouse passage turn right towards the lower ward. On the wall to your right (at the back of the shop), you will see the vertical grooves for portcullises [1], the springing of the vault over this smaller passage [2], and the holes in the wall which mark the position of the gudgeon pins from which the wooden gates were suspended.

Right: *Studying the detail at the back of the King's Gate, it becomes clear that the design was never fully completed. The numbers on this view highlight those features described in the tour text.*

Below: *The King's Gate is perhaps the most striking demonstration of the strength of medieval fortification in the British Isles.*

Near here is the access to the upper part of the gatehouse. A door on the right opens to a stair in the rearward part of the building [**3**]. This leads up to a wall-passage at first-floor level from which there is a modern footbridge across the north-west gate tower to the room above the main gate-passage [**4**]. Here a double *piscina* or sink in the east wall shows that this was a chapel, although because of its position not on the normal east–west orientation. Two of the portcullises rose up through the chapel floor, demonstrating that in a medieval castle the great gate was seldom open and then only for the briefest interval. The wall-passages at this level contain, in addition to a latrine to the left, arrowslits grouped in such a way that although only six openings are apparent from outside the castle, double that number of archers could discharge their shafts through them simultaneously.

Above the chapel, and the room in the tower on either side, there was to have been a large hall, 60 feet (18m) long [**5**]. The principal features of its north wall, apparently the only part to be completed, are three large two-light window seats [**6**], and over the gate two more groups of three-in-one arrowslits [**7**]. The projecting stone corbels for the roof supports are carved with what were once finely-decorated heads [**8**]. Having observed these features, you should now return to ground level.

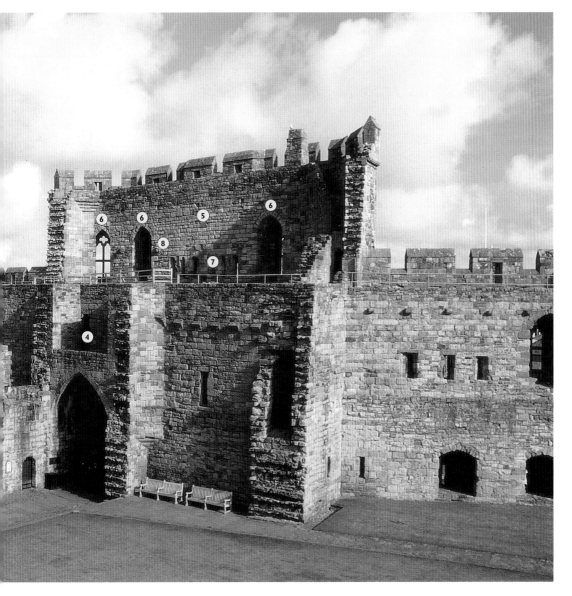

# THE KITCHENS

To the west (right) of the King's Gate lies the lower ward. Note the foundations of the broad wall which was intended to separate the two wards. Around the enclosing curtain walls, you will also see the foundations of the buildings which formerly occupied the ward; they would have concealed the lower parts of the curtain itself.

As you walk down towards the Eagle Tower you will come first, on your right, to the site of the castle kitchens, lying between the gatehouse and the Well Tower. The springer of a great arch and bonding for a cross partition wall, both built as part of the curtain wall, show that it was intended to build the whole in stone. But the slight foundation walls on the courtyard side suggest that, as built, these kitchens may have been relatively flimsy structures.

To the left of the range of three rooms are the remains of settings for two copper cauldrons, with fireplaces below them. Behind them, in the thickness of the tower wall, is a cavity which may have been used for smoking meat. At the bottom of the wall, on the right-hand side of this cavity, there is a small hole marking the end of a water channel running from a tank in the Well Tower, and below it there is a drain running off to the left.

In the window openings at the back of the range there is the line of a second channel, still bearing remains of its lead piping, running from the tower to a stone sink, now much weathered, mounted in a recess in the wall about the

*The seatings for two copper cauldrons, with fireplaces below, at the west end of the castle kitchens.*

middle of the range. In the wall below the great stone springer, on the right, is the small opening for a rubbish disposal shaft in the wall thickness. The accommodation at the right-hand end of these apartments was of two storeys; a doorway in the curtain wall opens on to a stair which served the upper room and the gatehouse.

*Cutaway section showing the tanks and channels which were originally supplied with water from the well in the Well Tower. The timber framing is merely a suggestion of the medieval form of the outer walls (Illustration by Chris Jones-Jenkins, 1996).*

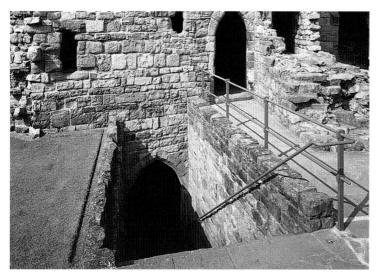

*The Well Tower could be entered from the courtyard at basement and ground-floor levels. The tower was of four storeys in all.*

## THE WELL TOWER

There are two entrances to the Well Tower from the courtyard, one at ground level, and the other leading into the basement. First, descend the steps to the latter, noting on the way down the position of the door which originally barred the entry. From the basement it is possible to obtain a 'cross-section' view of what was involved in the construction of all the ten major towers of the castle, for here none of the timber floors of the upper storeys have been restored, allowing the characteristic details of each room to be seen at a glance from below.

Including the basement, there were in all four storeys, and this was so in the majority of the northern towers. At basement level there is a wide gateway, once defended with outer and inner doors, portcullis and 'murder-holes'. This gateway was originally designed to allow water-borne supplies for the adjacent kitchens and service rooms to be brought in from the ditch (p. 44). At each of the three upper levels there is a pair of square holes on opposite sides of the tower, which, with supporting corbels below, carried the great cross-beams on which were laid the joists of the main floors. Each of these upper rooms has its own fireplace and its latrine reached by a passage in the thickness of the outside wall, arrangements which are common to practically all the rooms in the castle. The tower was left unfinished in the fourteenth century and much of its top, including the whole of the surmounting turret, is nineteenth-century work.

Return to ground level and re-enter the tower by the entrance near the top of the basement steps. From here a passage leads to the chamber containing the well which gives the tower its name; the well itself being almost 50 feet (15m) deep. Facing the well is a stone seating for a lead-lined cistern, which could be kept filled by buckets raised from the well, and from which ran inclined pipes in the thickness of the wall to the kitchens nearby. The well shaft extends upwards, allowing the water to be drawn at first-floor level.

Next to the well chamber, winding steps lead to the upper levels. At first-floor level, above the well chamber, there is a small room with a fireplace, possibly a little private kitchen. Also at this level, there is a wall-walk westwards to the Eagle Tower.

At the second-floor level there is a doorway intended to lead on to an upper wall-walk towards the Eagle Tower, but the curtain wall at this point was never carried above the first-floor stage. From the second-floor vestibule, steps lead up eastwards to the wall-walk on that side. At present, it can be followed at this level across the King's Gate, through the intervening towers, all the way to the North-East Tower. Finally, a newel staircase from the second-floor level also leads up to the restored battlements and the tower's surmounting turret.

*The ground-floor entrance to the Well Tower leads to the well chamber itself, seen to the right of this view. The well, covered by the modern grille, is nearly 50 feet (15m) deep.*

Back at ground level, you will see signs of a range of rooms against the curtain wall between the Well Tower and Eagle Tower. There is a restored fireplace, roof corbels and partition bonding stones representing these rooms. They were possibly never completed, or perhaps built with timber-framed walls.

# THE EAGLE TOWER

This is the greatest of all the castle's towers and was probably at first intended to provide accommodation for Sir Otto de Grandison, the king's lieutenant and first justiciar of north Wales. Everything about it is designed on a magnificent scale. Like the other northern towers it comprises a basement and three storeys, but there is more generous provision of wall-chambers and its group of three lofty turrets gives it special distinction.

The basement forms an ante-chamber through which anyone coming to Caernarfon by water would enter the castle. We, however, enter it by the steps leading down from the courtyard. The basement, like the three great rooms above, is ten-sided and measures some 30 to 35 feet (9 to 10.5m) across.

*A much-weathered stone eagle can still be recognized on the battlements of the west turret of the Eagle Tower.*

On the side opposite the entrance steps there is the passage leading in, through a portcullis and strongly-barred double door, from the waterside. From this passage, there are stairs communicating with the intended Water Gate (see p. 44). Another passage from the chamber would have given access to the basement of the buildings against the north curtain wall. With all the doors closed, the only natural light to come into the room would have been provided by a tall, single arrowloop at the face of a deep embrasure. At this point we can see the immense thickness of the tower walls — here about 18 feet (5.4m). A passage at one side of the embrasure led to a latrine.

The ground-floor room in the Eagle Tower is approached through a vestibule from the courtyard. Though dark, it is a room of noble proportions (at present occupied by an exhibition), and it is fitted with a large hooded fireplace. The floor and ceiling (the latter a close replica of the original arrangement) date from 1911–14, as do those elsewhere. Doors lead from this main chamber to passages and subsidiary chambers in the thickness of the walls. The little chamber opposite the entrance contained the gear for raising the portcullis of the postern gate below, while the

*A cutaway drawing revealing the internal arrangements of the Eagle Tower, viewed from the north-east (Illustration by Chris Jones-Jenkins, 1996).*

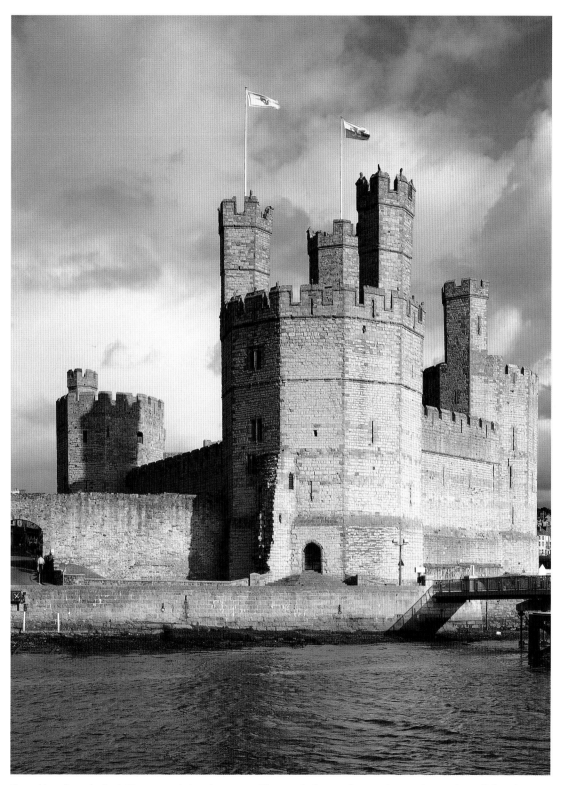

*Everything about the Eagle Tower was designed on a magnificent scale. Its grand proportions set it apart from all the other towers in the castle. From the outset, it was probably intended to provide accommodation for King Edward I's lieutenant in north Wales, Sir Otto de Grandison (1238–1328).*

passage to the right would have led to a room serving the same purpose over the adjacent Water Gate.

To the left of the entrance vestibule is the stair to the upper floors, and on the right, close to the foot, is a small octagonal chamber which was probably a chapel. The same arrangement occurs in similarly placed rooms in the Queen's and Chamberlain Towers.

The main chamber on the first floor, which currently houses a theatre, was originally the principal apartment of the tower and is like that below but better lit. There is the same elaborate provision of accommodation in the thickness of the walls, with the south-east angle occupied, as on the floors below, by an octagonal chapel; here the purpose is made certain by the remains of a trefoil-headed *piscina* — a stoup for holy water.

To the right of the entrance vestibule, a passage leads to a small rectangular room traditionally, but almost certainly wrongly, identified as the birthplace of the first English prince of Wales. If, by the time of his birth in April 1284, the walls of the Eagle Tower had been built to this height, the main chamber would surely be the more likely location. Inserted in the window of the small room are the arms of Albert Edward, prince of Wales, afterwards King Edward VII (1901–10). For a time at least the tower did not extend above this level, the second floor and watch towers above being fourteenth-century additions; note the evidence of this in the central chamber where the up-and-down slope of the offset where the ceiling rests on the walls shows that they were at first built to take a low-pitched outer roof at this point.

The topmost room, entered directly from the stair, is well lit by a pair of two-light windows, both with stepped window-seats, and there is a large fireplace. There are rectangular wall chambers on the north and north-east, the latter perhaps a kitchen, while a passage on the south leads to a latrine.

The main stair leads on up to the roof of the tower, and from here to the top of the most westerly of the three turrets. The battlements, both on the tower and on the turrets, are unrestored, and their copings preserve the remains of the numerous stone figures with which they were originally decorated. Some of these were evidently helmeted heads, while on the west turret an eagle — although much weathered — is still recognizable. Remains of similar stone figures will be noticed in other parts of the castle.

# THE CASTLE ACCOMMODATION

*In this late fourteenth-century French manuscript illustration, a king and his entourage are seen approaching a walled town. The accommodation at Caernarfon was designed to house such a large royal household when the occasion demanded (By kind permission of the British Library, Harley Ms. 4372, f. 79v).*

Whilst traversing the wall-passages, climbing the stairs, and viewing some of the great rooms at Caernarfon Castle, we may well wonder why the castle was built here and on so vast a scale. We may be curious, too, about why so many rooms were provided and who was to use them. The answers are touched upon elsewhere in this guide (pp. 38–9).

We should remember that Caernarfon was to be the capital of a new dominion and the palace of a new dynasty of princes. It had to be capable, when occasion required, of adequately accommodating the household of the king's eldest son, with his council, his family, his guests and all who attended on them. This also implies the capacity to store the treasure, the wardrobe, the records, the provender, the supplies of all kinds required to sustain a great medieval household in appropriate state, as well as to accommodate such officials as the constable and the watchmen, together with a small garrison, whose presence in the castle was a permanency.

History, in the event, seldom if ever fulfilled for the castle the high role intended for it, and in practice, in the fourteenth century at any rate, it had little more to do than serve as the depot for the armament and building maintenance of the other north Wales castles.

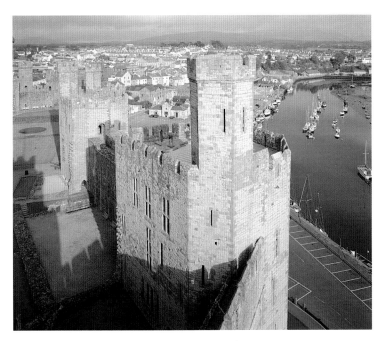

This view, from the top of the Eagle Tower, shows the Queen's Tower (Banner Tower) with the Chamberlain Tower beyond. Against the curtain wall between these two southern towers are the foundations of the Great Hall.

# THE GREAT HALL

Against the wall between the Queen's and Chamberlain Towers was the 100 feet long (30.5m) Great Hall. Although little more than foundations survive, the quality of the masonry at the west (right-hand) end with its fine moulded plinth, shows that, when complete, this must have been a splendid building. The high table would have been to the right, the screens passage, buttery and pantry presumably to the left, where there are now steps leading down to a postern gate. The hall was connected directly to the Chamberlain Tower by a door at the south-east corner.

# THE QUEEN'S TOWER

The regimental museum of the Royal Welch Fusiliers now occupies the Queen's Tower and two floors of the Chamberlain Tower. The museum is entered from the ground floor of the Chamberlain Tower and information panels in the upper wall passage, accessed from the first-floor chamber, lead the visitor through a 'one-way' circuit to further displays in the Queen's Tower.

The Queen's Tower is linked to the Eagle Tower by a length of curtain with wall-walks at two levels, the lower evidently intended to be completed as a covered passage like those further to the east. Against this wall there has been a building of which only foundations survive. The two towers have common internal dimensions and wall thicknesses, but here there are only three storeys. On the right, at the north-west corner of the tower, there is a spiral stair from the courtyard to the roof, which communicated with the two upper rooms and their encircling wall-passages. The wall-walk, accessible from the roof of the tower, and the lower wall passage can be followed the full length of the south curtain to the Queen's Gate. Each floor also has subsidiary rooms at the north-east corner, of which the topmost was certainly, and each of the others probably, a chapel. A modern timber staircase has been erected in the space formerly occupied by these rooms.

The roof turret is rather larger than the others in the castle, and at half height has a small hexagonal chamber from which a narrow flight of steps continues to the summit. A lintel above these steps contains a round hole for the base of a flag-staff, a reminder that this tower was called *Tour de la Banere* — Banner Tower — in the fourteenth century.

When complete, the Great Hall at Caernarfon must have been a splendid building, and would have been the scene of lavish entertainment. In this thirteenth-century French manuscript illustration, a king and queen entertain at the high table in just such a hall (By permission of the British Library, Royal Ms. 14 E III, f. 89).

# THE CHAMBERLAIN TOWER

One should enter this tower by the ground-floor entrance (signposted for the museum of the Royal Welch Fusiliers). The Chamberlain Tower (also called at different times the Treasury Tower and the Record Tower) is smaller than those previously described, and contains three 22 feet (6.7m) wide octagonal rooms.

The two lower floors now house the museum of the Royal Welch Fusiliers. Annexed to the north-east angle of each room are rectangular chambers, that on the first floor serving as a chapel. These small chambers are now used as offices. The second-floor chamber currently houses an exhibition. Continuous wall-passages circle the outer sides of the tower at first- and second-floor levels, which link with the upper wall-passage and wall walks to west and east.

*The lower wall-passage between the Chamberlain and Queen's Towers.*

From the second floor, the stair leads to the roof and from there to the top of the turret. The battlements and cresting of the tower proper are original, those of the turret restored. The only surviving stone chimney in the castle is the one on the leads at the back of the turret.

Between the Chamberlain Tower and the Black Tower, the wall-passages continue within the curtain. That on the first floor is now unroofed, but was certainly intended to form a covered gallery like the one below. Above is an open wall-walk at battlement level. The change in direction which the curtain makes mid-way between the towers arises from the fact that at this point it crosses the line of the ditch of the Norman motte.

*A cutaway drawing of the curtain wall as it runs west from the Chamberlain Tower. The drawing gives an indication of the form of the Great Hall which stood against the wall at this point. The principal arrangements included wall-passages at two levels and, a wall-walk above, with the arrangements repeated to the east of the tower. Continuous wall-passages also circle the outer face of the tower itself (Illustration by Chris Jones-Jenkins, 1996).*

# THE BLACK TOWER AND THE CISTERN TOWER

There is no access at ground level to either of these towers, so to reach them you should enter the doorway to the left of the Chamberlain Tower and make your way along the lower wall-passage. This is the only passage along this part of the wall that does not come to a dead end at the Queen's Gate.

The Black Tower contains two small ten-sided rooms, one above the other, instead of the usual three or four. This was partly because it was built against the side of the motte, so that much of what appears as tower externally is in fact a solid foundation revetting the made ground of the earlier earthwork. There are subsidiary rooms opening off the central chamber at each level, of which the upper, now floorless, consisted of an ante-chapel with a chapel to the east of it.

The stair in the north-west corner of the tower gives access to this upper floor, to the roof leads and to the surmounting turret. Short flights of steps continue the wall-walk across the leads from one side of the tower to the other, an arrangement not found elsewhere in the castle and it is possible that it was intended to add a third storey to the tower bringing its height up to that of the Queen's Gate. These upper flights of stairs would then have been replaced by a level wall-passage similar to that on the floor below.

As with the Black Tower, a door opens directly from the ground-floor passage into the lower part of the Cistern Tower, which at this level contains a small hexagonal chamber with three arrowloops towards the south.

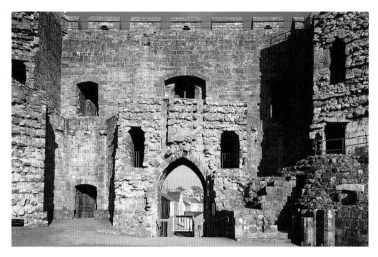

*The back of the Queen's Gate was one of those parts of the castle which was never fully completed. Its design can be appreciated, almost in 'cross-section'.*

Above the vault there is an open, stone-lined rainwater tank from which the tower takes it name. This can be seen from the wall-walk which may be reached by one of the narrow stairs leading up from the embrasures of the middle (unroofed) passage of curtain.

A stone outlet channel, which runs through the thickness of the wall, and discharges through a shaft in the Queen's Gate, will be noticed crossing one of the nearby arrowloops. The top of the tower appears unfinished and would no doubt have been carried up to match the level of the top of the Queen's Gate.

# THE QUEEN'S GATE

The ground-floor passage from the Cistern Tower leads to the Queen's Gate. This second great gateway into the castle was never finished and, seen from within, it can therefore be viewed in 'cross-section'. The unusual character of the external façade, and the elevated position of the gate-passage — high above the street outside — was dictated by the height of the earlier medieval

motte, against which this part of the castle was raised. Originally, the gate would have been approached from outside by a great stone-built ramp with gently graded steps.

Seen on plan, the gatehouse consists of a central passage and bridge pit flanked by polygonal towers. At ground level each tower contained an irregularly shaped porter's room, the northern of which still remains open to the courtyard.

The lofty position of this gate made it less vulnerable than the King's Gate and its defences are in consequence less elaborate. There was a drawbridge (or, more correctly, a 'turning' bridge), and on either side can be seen the bearings for the roller on which it pivoted. Below is a deep pit which took the counterpoise weight when the bridge was in the raised position. Above, the vault was well provided with 'murder-holes'; you can see five, two of them showing in section towards the courtyard. To the rear of the gate-passage, and slightly to the south of it, an inner gate and portcullis was planned. Above the gate there was to be a wall-passage connecting the passages in the curtain walls to north and south.

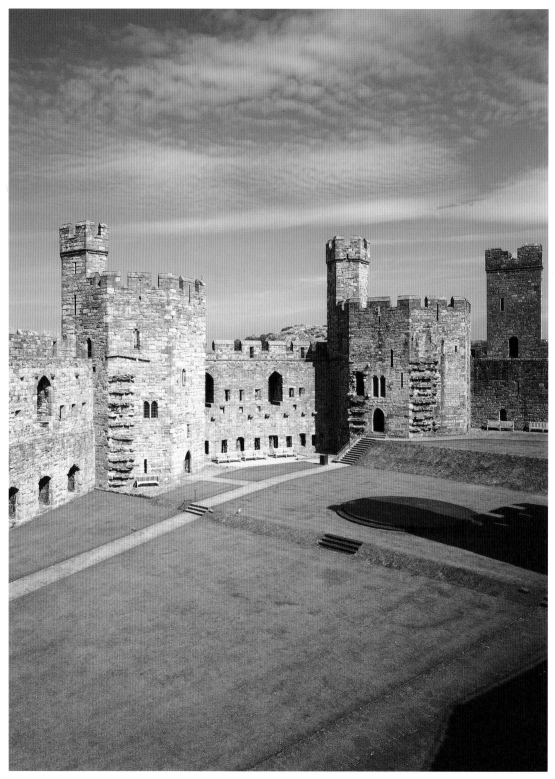

*In this general view across the upper ward of the castle, the Granary Tower appears to the left, the North-East Tower in the centre distance, with the slender Watch Tower to the right. The shape of the ward as a whole was largely determined by the great mound of the Norman castle which lay in this area.*

This can be seen in section on either side where the backs of the gatehouse towers have been left unfinished. At this upper level it was intended that there should be a hall extending, as over the King's Gate, across the full width of the gatehouse.

## THE WATCH TOWER

Had the Queen's Gate been completed, the wall-passage in the short section of curtain wall between the gate and the North-East Tower would have connected with the corresponding passage in the south curtain. This passage can only be entered from the North-East Tower. The wall-walk above also comes to a dead end at the Queen's Gate.

From the wall-walk a doorway led to the upper part of the slender turret now known as the Watch Tower. The top was a look-out point with a lean-to roof to give cover to the watchman. The battlements both here and on the nearby wall-walk retain traces of the grooves in which were hung wooden shutters for the protection of the crossbowmen.

## THE NORTH-EAST TOWER

This is an octagonal tower of two storeys only. The ground-floor room houses an exhibition on the princes of Wales. The characteristic wall-passages of the southern curtain are continued round the outer sides of the tower, but do not go beyond it. This is because the work of the earlier building period terminates here and wall-passages were not provided in the northern curtain which, from this point to the Eagle Tower, dated from 1295 and later. The stair is at the north-west corner and ascends to the top of the turret. The battlements of this turret are unusual in having arrowloops set beneath them.

*A close-up view of one of the multiple arrowslits between the Granary Tower and the North-East Tower.*

## THE GRANARY TOWER

In many respects the Granary Tower duplicates the Well Tower. It is octagonal, of four storeys surmounted by a turret, and has a wall-passage at ground level leading to a well chamber. Of the main rooms, only the top floor, which is unroofed, is accessible to visitors. It is crossed by the wall-walk along the top of the curtain which can be followed across the King's Gate to the Well Tower and so down to the courtyard again.

One of the most interesting features in the castle is the multiple grouping of arrowslits at two levels in the curtain wall on either side of the Granary Tower. These represent a refinement of the arrangements noted in the upper floors of the King's Gate (p. 27). The fire power which these loops enabled to be brought to bear on a limited front must — by medieval standards — have been devastating.

Below: *A cutaway section showing how the castle's multiple arrowslits may have been used (Illustration by Chris Jones-Jenkins, 1996).*

## THE NORTH FACE OF THE CASTLE

Leaving the castle through the King's Gate, note the various defensive features mentioned at the beginning of the tour. Looking back at it from the bridge outside, you will see above the entrance the much weathered statue of King Edward II, the first English prince of Wales. We know the statue was erected in 1321, and it is a reminder that this side of the castle formed part of the second phase of the castle's history. It was raised after the original defences had been overrun during the Welsh revolt of 1294.

After crossing the bridge, turn right along Castle Ditch. This ditch was originally twice as wide as it is now, and would have isolated the castle from the town. On reaching the angle tower opposite the beginning of the town wall, you will see that the dark bands of stone on the face of the tower stop to its right, marking the change of build between work executed before (to the left) and after (to the right) 1295. At this point, the castle ditch linked to another bordering the town wall and continued past

# THE PURPOSE OF THE TOWN AND CASTLE

*King Edward I saw his borough at Caernarfon as a nucleus of English influence and the administrative centre for the new shire counties of north-west Wales. There had been little change in the structure of the town when it was mapped by John Speed in 1610 (By courtesy of the National Library of Wales).*

When Edward I began to build the walled town of Caernarfon in 1283, and issued its charter of privileges in the following year, his object was to create a nucleus of English influence which could adapt a place famous in Welsh story and with great natural advantages to conditions brought about by the success of his armies. An early draft of the Statute of Wales shows that even before it was decided to form a county of Caernarvonshire, Caernarfon had been selected as the administrative centre for the lands subsequently grouped in the new shires of Caernarvon, Anglesey and Merioneth. The justiciar and chamberlain of north Wales, established to administer the judicial and financial systems of the principality thus annexed to the English crown, accordingly had their offices in Caernarfon; there the courts were held for the three shires, and there the justiciar had his chief official residence. Within the county organization, the sheriff, the coroners, and other local officers were based there.

The new town provided quarters and protection for all these officials, their deputies, clerks and assistants; for the builders and craftsmen who worked on the castle; and for a small maritime and mercantile community who maintained contact with the other English coastal towns in Wales, with England itself through Chester and Bristol, and with the king's possessions in Ireland and Gascony. The rights and privileges prescribed in the charter were intended to attract to a distant and lately hostile land, settlers who, by following these callings, would aid the working out of government policy and the gradual pacification of the country.

Anyone familiar with the other great castles of north Wales — Conwy, Harlech, Beaumaris, Flint, Rhuddlan and Aberystwyth — will have noticed that their round towers give them a certain family resemblance which at Caernarfon is apparent only in the town wall. Here the castle is plainly a building apart, wearing an aspect of nobility all its own. This is chiefly derived from its spacious multangular towers, which must already have been commissioned in 1283, the year in which their foundations were laid. Thus the castle would seem to have been marked out for a special role even before the birth, within its precinct, of the first English prince of Wales.

the Queen's Gate to the River Seiont. The town wall proper did not cross the castle ditch, but terminated at its edge, and the smooth vertical face of its upper section can still be seen. From this point a lower and less massive wall was carried down to the full depth of the ditch and across to the castle.

Those not wishing to visit the town walls should turn left after

crossing the bridge and make their way along the ditch to the arch in the wall. Shortly before reaching the Eagle Tower, note the break in the coursing of the masonry and the termination of the bands of darker stone which again mark the change of build between work executed before (to the right) and after (to the left) 1295. Beyond the arch lies the River Seiont, to the left, the castle car-park.

*The statue of King Edward II, the first English prince of Wales, was erected above the King's Gate in 1321.*

---

Late in 1285 or early in 1286 the constableship of Caernarfon was granted to the king's closest friend and adviser Sir Otto de Grandison (1238–1328), a Savoyard nobleman from Grandson on Lake Neuchâtel, of whom Edward said, 'there was no one about him who could do his will better'. To this same Otto had already been given the highest appointment of all, that of justiciar of north Wales,

a post equivalent to that of viceroy and carrying an annual fee of £1,000. Thus, as soon as its building was well advanced, this particular castle was put in charge of the king's special confidant and lieutenant, who drew the constable's salary of £100 and retained at least nominal custody for the next four years.

We cannot tell how early the decision was taken that the king would eventually confer the principality on one of his sons. Certainly it looks very much as if, at the time the design for the castle was being prepared in 1283, it was already in view as the future official residence of the king's representative in the principality, who, if all went well, would be a prince of Edward's house. Such a purpose would

demand a building of specially imposing character — a building which, though fortified with all and more than all the strength of the other castles, might yet have the appearance of a palace. It is most likely for this reason that Caernarfon's towers were not only shaped, but also decorated with broad bands of different-coloured stone, so as to resemble one of the best-known monuments of imperial Rome, namely the city walls of Constantinople.

*With its multangular towers and decorative stone banding, Caernarfon stands apart from Edward I's other great castles in north Wales. The inspiration may have come from these fifth-century Roman walls at Constantinople — the modern city of Istanbul (Photograph by Martin Hürlimann).*

*In 1285–86, King Edward I granted the constableship of Caernarfon to his closest friend and adviser, Sir Otto de Grandison (1238–1328). A Savoyard nobleman, Otto was to be buried in Lausanne Cathedral, Switzerland, where this tomb effigy can still be seen (Photograph by Claude Bornand, courtesy of Daniel de Raemy).*

# A TOUR OF THE TOWN WALLS

The circuit of walls and towers enclosing the medieval borough has survived unbroken. It extends from near the north-east to near the north-west corner of the castle, a distance of about 800 yards (734m). There are eight towers and two twin-towered gateways at intervals of approximately 70 yards (21m).

## THE NORTH-EAST CORNER OF THE CASTLE TO THE EAST GATE

From Castle Ditch to the East Gate there are three sections of wall and two intervening towers. Before following Greengate Street along the outside of the wall, turn into Hole in the Wall Street to look at the inside face, where there are the slight remains of one of the stairs which gave access to the wall-walk and to the upper floor of the adjacent tower. The stair has the effect of doubling the thickness of the wall, which is here pierced by a postern

gate, formerly closed by a portcullis as well as by wooden doors. Although the inner face of Tower 1 nearby has been stripped, it is still possible to see a sloping line of holes which show that when it was built an inclined scaffold ramp was used.

Return to Greengate Street, so called because the postern was known as the Green Gate from its proximity to the Green (now Castle Square), and follow it along to Tower 2, which still stands to the full height of the battlements. On either side of it may be seen the fragments of the stone revetment originally built to

Above: *The early fourteenth-century seal of the borough of Caernarfon (By courtesy of the Society of Antiquaries).*

Left: *The circuit of walls and towers enclosing the medieval borough survives almost complete. The stretch of wall facing the Menai Strait was from the outset the town quay, and still retains something of its medieval atmosphere.*

retain the steep banks which foot the adjoining stretch of wall (the interior of the tower can be seen from an alley off Hole in the Wall Street). The wall from here to the East Gate (3) has been largely refaced with pinkish stone which is more regularly coursed than, and therefore easily distinguishable from, the original masonry.

## THE EAST GATE

*The East Gate, also known as the Exchequer Gate, was the main landward entry into the medieval borough. The rooms above the gateway served from the first to accommodate the exchequer, the financial and administrative centre for Edward I's new shire counties in north-west Wales.*

This was the principal landward entrance to the town. Here Greengate Street passes under a stone bridge which incorporates the final arch of a medieval bridge, which was built in 1301 to carry the approach to the walled town across the low-lying River Cadnant (which is now culverted over). It consisted of five stone arches with a timber drawbridge in front of the gate. As this drawbridge was under repair in 1520, it cannot have been replaced by the present stone arch earlier

than the sixteenth century. From below it is possible to see the original width of the bridge, part of which has been exposed to the right beyond the arch. As built in the 1280s, the bridge was a wooden structure; this was destroyed by the rebels in 1294–95, and its rebuilding in stone was put in hand in 1301 or 1302.

In front of the main gate there was originally a smaller, battlemented gateway where the tolls on merchandise were collected; this was connected to the main gate by a drawbridge across the town ditch. The rooms above the main gateway served from the first to accommodate the exchequer, established by the Statute of Wales (1284) as the administrative and financial centres of the counties of Caernarvon, Anglesey and Merioneth. The gateway was altered in 1767 to become the Town Hall, and in 1873 the Guildhall; it incorporates much relatively modern work, but the remains of the twin medieval gate towers can still be seen in their proper relationship to the adjacent walls.

*A drawing of the East Gate in 1791, by G. J. Farrington. The stone bridge represents the last arch of the 1301 construction which carried the approach road to the walled town across the River Cadnant (By courtesy of the Victoria and Albert Museum).*

## FROM THE EAST GATE TO THE WATERFRONT

Beyond the East Gate is an angle tower (4) standing to the full height of its battlements, which retain their cresting with the remains of finials. The length of wall between this and the next tower (5) is the best preserved of all. Here the battlements contain the bases of arrowslits rising well-defined above the level of the wall-walk. The opening to Northgate Street is relatively modern, as are those to Market Street and Church Street.

*The section of town wall between Tower 4 and Tower 5 is the best preserved stretch of the defences. The battlements rise above the level of the wall-walk and retain the bases of several arrowslits.*

*In 1303, Edward of Caernarfon licensed Henry of Ellerton 'to build a chantry chapel in the town of Carnarvan on his burgage there'. This marks the foundation of the chapel of St Mary, in the north-west corner of the town walls. It was always a chapel of ease to the mother church at Llanbeblig.*

Between Towers 5 and 6 the wall still retains some of the whitening applied to its surface at the back of the buildings which, until the 1930s, entirely screened it from view.

The early fourteenth-century chapel of St Mary is built against the inside of the wall beyond Tower 6; the angle tower (7) is incorporated in it and served as its vestry. Initially, the new borough was served by Llanbeblig church, but in 1303 Edward, prince of Wales, licensed Henry of Ellerton 'to build a chantry chapel in the town of Carnarvan on his burgage there'. The church has been much restored, but the arcades are original early fourteenth-century features.

Within the wall, on the opposite side of Church Street, is another of the stone stairs. This provides public access to a short length of wall-walk. The inner faces of Towers 4 and 6 are well preserved, together with their bridges which were originally of timber, subsequently replaced by stone. In 1347 the then chamberlain of north Wales was ordered 'to repair the bridges on the walls of the said town ... so that it may be possible to walk safely on the walls and defend the town in case of peril'. Tower 5, like Tower 1, has lost all its interior facework.

# FROM THE NORTH-WEST CORNER TO THE CASTLE

The towers on this side of the town are occupied and inaccessible to visitors, but this long stretch of wall facing the Menai Strait still retains its medieval atmosphere in a way that is denied to the parts engulfed by the growth of the later town. Here from the beginning was the quay. Originally it was constructed of wood, but it was burned in the troubles of 1294–95, and was rebuilt in stone in the early fourteenth century. In the eighteenth century the southern part of what is now the Anglesey Hotel was the Custom House.

Just to the south of Tower 7, a blocked doorway is visible. Originally, before the building of St Mary's chapel, a postern gate stood here but the arch was subsequently moved a few feet to form the west door of the chapel. It was blocked up later as a protective measure.

The door, windows, battlements and castellated chimney of Tower 8 are nineteenth-century additions, as are the windows and battlements of the West Gate (9), which consists of a twin-towered gatehouse with a small projecting barbican, and which houses the Royal Welsh Yacht Club. The portcullis grooves still survive in part and there is a fragment of a projecting latrine at wall-walk level just to the left of the left-hand tower. A sixteenth-century record refers to it as the 'Gildyn Yeate' or Golden Gate, and in Welsh it is still the 'Porth-yr-Aur'.

Tower 10, which preserves an arrowslit on the left side, is occupied in connection with the adjacent County Offices into which the nineteenth-century buildings of the former County Gaol have been converted. The presence of the Police Station (1853) and the County Hall (1863), the latter containing the Crown Court, recalls the fact that the administration of justice has been carried out on this site for over seven centuries.

At the west end of the castle ditch the town wall is pierced by a relatively modern archway on the site of an older and narrower postern, remains of which can be seen to the right of the existing opening.

*The twin-towered West Gate was referred to in a sixteenth-century document as the 'Gildyn Yeate' — the Golden Gate. In Welsh it is still the 'Porth-yr-Aur'.*

The continuation of the wall from this arch at full height across to the castle was not part of the original plan and dates to 1326. The intention of the thirteenth-century builders was to erect against this side of the Eagle Tower a great Water Gate through which — had it ever been completed — water-borne supplies could have been carried at high tide to the door in the basement of the Well Tower. Note the evidence for this on the left side of the Eagle Tower where there are still to be seen the slot for a portcullis, the springers and jambs of the great arch and two doorways in the face of the tower itself, one above the other. The doors would have provided access to the accommodation above the gate.

Before passing round to the south side of the castle, return to the modern archway and pass through it into Castle Ditch. Just to the left of the Eagle Tower you will see a break in the coursing of the masonry and the termination of the bands of darker stone. This marks the change of build between work executed before (to the right) and after (to the left) 1295.

Returning through the arch and continuing round the Eagle Tower you will pass the entry to the tower basement, with its portcullis and strongly-barred double doors.

Further along the southern façade, between the Chamberlain and Black Towers, a change in the alignment of the curtain wall marks the position of the ditch which encircled the base of the Norman motte. Indications of the presence of the motte itself appear in the sloping apron or revetment of stone which begins to rise at this point and continues past the Queen's Gate to the North-East Tower. The different angles at which the walls run were governed partly by the existence of this earlier fortification, and partly by the need to provide covering and cross-fire over every part of the ground below the castle.

The overall effect of this splendid façade, with its continuous bands of darker-coloured stone, can best be gained by crossing the river.

*The best position to appreciate the splendid southern façade of the castle, with its multangular towers and banded walls, is from across the River Seiont.*

### FURTHER READING

P. J. Casey and J. L. Davies with J. Evans, *Excavations at Segontium (Caernarfon) Roman Fort, 1975–1979* (CBA Research Report 90, London 1993).

R. R. Davies, *Conquest, Coexistence, and Change: Wales 1063–1415* (Oxford 1987); reprinted in paperback as, *The Age of Conquest: Wales 1063–1415* (Oxford 1991).

T. P. Ellis and John Lloyd, editors, *The Mabinogion: A New Translation*, 2 vols (Oxford 1929), I, 133-50: 'The Dream of Macsen Wledig'.

J. Goronwy Edwards, 'Edward I's Castle-Building in Wales', *Proceedings of the British Academy*, **32** (1946), 15–81.

Charles Kightly, *Caernarfon: A Royal Palace in Wales* (Cardiff 1991).

C. R. Peers. 'Carnarvon Castle', *Transactions of the Honourable Society of Cymmrodorion* (1915–16), 1–74.

Michael Prestwich, *Edward I* (London 1988).

Royal Commission on Ancient and Historical Monuments in Wales and Monmouthshire, *An Inventory of the Ancient Monuments in Caernarvonshire, Volume II: Central* (London 1960), 124–56.

A. J. Taylor, 'The Birth of Edward of Caernarvon and the Beginnings of Caernarvon Castle', *History*, new series, **35** (1950), 256–61.

A. J. Taylor, 'The Date of Caernarvon Castle', *Antiquity*, **26** (1952), 25–34.

A. J. Taylor, *Caernarvon Castle and Town Wall* (HMSO, London 1953).

A. J. Taylor, 'Castle-Building in Thirteenth-Century Wales and Savoy', *Proceedings of the British Academy*, **63** (1977), 265–92.

Arnold Taylor, *Four Great Castles* (Newtown 1983).

Arnold Taylor, *The Welsh Castles of Edward I* (London 1986).